To Nana and Mom —B.H.

Text copyright © 2017 by Bridget Heos
Illustrations copyright © 2017 by David Clark

hmhco.com

The illustrations in this book were done in pen and ink, watercolor, and digital media.

The text type was set in Agenda and Felt-Tip Woman.
The display type was hand-lettered by David Clark.

The Library of Congress has cataloged the paper over board edition as follows:
Heos, Bridget, author.
Just like us!, birds / by Bridget Heos.
pages cm.
Summary: "Just Like Us! Birds gives young readers an up-close and personal look at how birds
do things that are remarkably similar to the way humans do." — Provided by publisher.
Audience: Ages 4–8.
Audience: K to grade 3.
Includes bibliographical references.
1. Birds—Juvenile literature. 2. Birds—Behavior—Juvenile literature. 3. Birds—Migration—Juvenile literature. I. Title. II. Title: Birds.
QL676.2.H457 2016
598—dc23
2015018893

ISBN: 978-0-544-57044-3 paper over board
ISBN: 978-0-358-00386-1 paperback

Printed in Malaysia
TWP 10 9 8 7 6 5 4 3 2 1
4500748804

Lexile Level	Guided Reading	Fountas & Pinnell	Interest Level
980	R	P	Grades K–2

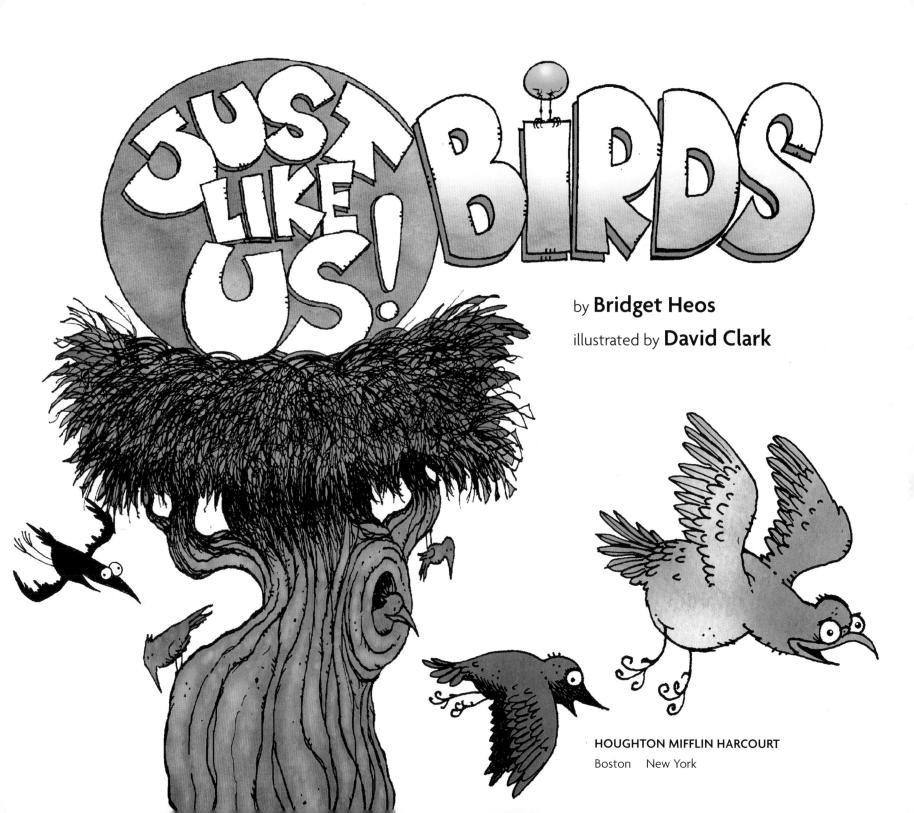

JUST LIKE US! BIRDS

by **Bridget Heos**

illustrated by **David Clark**

HOUGHTON MIFFLIN HARCOURT

Boston   New York

Sing a Song

BIRDS CAN SING up to one hundred notes in two seconds, compared to the twenty-eight sung by the world's fastest rapper. The human ear can't even hear all those notes!

And while a crow's song is less than lovely, European blackbird songs have been compared to classical music, complete with major and minor notes. No matter how melodic, male birds do most of the singing—and are telling other males that a territory is taken.

Baby Talk

BIRDS LEARN TO SING in the same way that babies begin to talk. First the chicks "babble," singing random notes that are like a baby's "googoo gaga." Then they sing parts of songs incorrectly, much like a human toddler saying, "My want milk." Finally, they graduate to singing songs correctly.

Rockin' Out Being a talented singer has its advantages. A bird that can sing multiple songs can trick would-be intruders into thinking that more than one bird is present and ready to defend the territory. Human rock stars can keep their screaming fans. Birds would rather sing to an empty tree!

Sound FX

BIRDS ARE NOT JUST good singers. They're also experts at creating sound effects to help defend their territory. And a bird that can secure a good territory is quite a catch for a female bird! For this reason, the male lyrebird imitates twenty different birds in its mating song, and occasionally throws in the sound of a camera shutter, a car alarm, or a chainsaw (you know, for romance).

A Couple of Geniuses While visiting his neighborhood pet store, Mozart heard a bird whistling a section of his Concerto No. 17 in G Major, which he had just written a month before (and kept quite secret from the public). So how did the bird learn the tune? The bird may have composed the tune independently. Or Mozart may have visited the store whistling or humming the tune and the bird picked up on it. Either way, Mozart took the fellow musical genius home, and the bird became his beloved pet.

What a Flirt!

ONCE A MALE HAS A TERRITORY, he needs to find a mate. Just like some humans, birds flirt to attract one another. Some offer gifts. An arctic tern flies over the colony, fish in mouth. The female bird follows behind until he finds the right spot to present such a romantic gift. Terns mate for life, so the fish serves as a wedding ring of sorts. With this fish, I thee wed!

With this fish, I thee wed.

Come Dancing.

MANY BIRDS DO ELABORATE DANCES to attract the eyes of someone special. When the bird of paradise spreads its wings, it no longer looks like a bird but more like a cartoon character because of the blue markings on the undersides of its wings. Then it does a flamenco-style dance.

MALE BOWERBIRDS BUILD bachelor pads known as bowers. These are not nests, for they are not used for laying eggs. They are built only to attract a mate. The male decorates the bower with flowers, feathers, berries, and fine art such as drinking straws, bottle caps, and plastic milk rings. The bowerbird is quite the interior designer, moving a flower, hopping back to see how it looks, and then rearranging it. But style varies by species. Some paint their bowers with their beaks, using charcoal or crushed berries as paint, and others decorate entirely in blue.

NEST SWEET NEST

ONCE TWO BIRDS PAIR UP, they build nests—in many shapes and sizes. Eagle nests stand ten feet tall and weigh more than two tons, a far cry from the cozy nest of the hummingbird. Just as a human parent swaddles a baby in a soft blanket, the hummingbird mother chooses only the softest materials for her nest. She gathers thistle petals, dandelion down, hair, feathers, and even laundry lint, and glues it all together with soft, spongy spider webs. Then she camouflages the outside with lichen and bark so that predators can't see it.

Knitting a Nest

BIRDS ARE EXPERTS AT SEWING and weaving. Northern orioles gather plant fibers, along with string and yarn left behind by humans. The female ties the fibers to the twigs on a tree. Then, using her beak as a needle, she knits the nest, using thousands of stitches, knots, and loops, until it resembles an upside-down stocking cap. The nest is strong, yet stretchy enough to expand as her chicks hatch and grow.

Egg-Cellent Parenting

ONCE THE NEST IS MADE, it's time to lay the eggs—and keep them warm. At this point, some moms are on their own. Chickens, ducks, and hummingbirds are all successful single mothers. When there are two parents, however, they often take turns brooding the eggs. Sometimes the less colorful female stays in the nest while the bright-feathered male hunts for food. Unlike her red mate, a cardinal mama is brownish like the nest. That way, predators don't see her while she protects the babies.

Once they hatch, bird babies keep their parents busy, just like human babies! The cardinal daddy feeds them insects about eight times an hour during daylight. After a couple days of keeping her featherless young warm, mama helps hunt for baby food too. The cardinals are so set on filling their babies' bellies that they sometimes get mixed up and feed babies in other nests, or other species altogether, even goldfish in a pond!

Emperor Penguin Dads Rule

EMPEROR PENGUIN DADS BROOD the eggs while the moms bring home the bacon—er, fish! It's not your average business trip. After laying the egg, the mother must travel seventy miles across ice to get to the ocean, where she'll dive deep into the icy sea for fish, squid, and krill. Meanwhile, Dad balances the egg on his feet, holding it against his warm belly. The stay-at-Antarctica dad remains like this for sixty-four days with nothing to eat, even as temperatures sometimes dip to 80 degrees below zero.

Got (crop) Milk?

AT LAST, MAMA RETURNS! And just in time. The egg has hatched, and chickie is hungry! Just as human babies drink milk, penguin chicks drink something called crop milk. But it's not really milk. It's throw-up. The mama has eaten her fill of fish. Now she spits it back up into her baby's beak. Fish puke—it does the body good!

DIRTY Diapers

BESIDES FEEDING THEM, parents clean up after their babies—by changing diapers! Birds need to keep their nests poop-free so as not to attract microbes and insects. But their babies aren't potty-trained yet. Luckily, baby poop comes in a diaper of sorts called a fecal sac. The parents carry these birdie diapers off and drop them. Or in some cases, eat them, which is not like us at all!

FAKER!

PARENT BIRDS ALSO HAVE to protect their young. Some fly at would-be nest raiders to frighten them away, but a little trickery sometimes works better. If a predator approaches a killdeer's nest, a parent killdeer will fly to the ground and flap its wing as though hurt. To the would-be nest raider, the adult bird looks like an easy target—and a bigger meal than the babies. The fooled predator follows, but the killdeer stays one step ahead. When far enough from the babies, the killdeer flies off, having successfully pulled the wool—er, feathers—over the predator's eyes.

BiRDie SEE, BiRDie Do!

BIRD PARENTS ALSO TEACH their youngsters important lessons. And just like human kids, chicks learn by watching. For instance, children watch their parents cook and then pretend to cook with their toys. Crow parents hide food to retrieve later. Their children copy them, hiding their "toys"—sticks, stones, and acorn caps.

FASTEST ANIMAL IN THE WORLD!

IN TIME, BABY BIRDS GROW UP and learn to find their own food—but there aren't any bird supermarkets. The peregrine falcon learns to soar above waterways until its prey—a duck—is within range. Then, with skills rivaling a fighter pilot's, it folds its wings and dives down at speeds of up to 200 miles per hour—making it not only the fastest bird on earth, but the fastest animal. At the last second, it lowers its feet and catches the duck with its talons.

Gone Fishin'! Instead of hunting, a heron fishes. It puts out bait like human fishers do and then lies in wait. Insects and bread bits are used as bait, and feathers and sticks as lures. The heron tosses these objects in the water, and when fish come to see what's up, the bird stabs the fish with its beak.

Winging It...

MANY BIRDS put their flying skills to another use—migrating. These birds travel great distances across land or sea to reach their winter homes. Large birds such as ducks and geese travel by day, following landmarks like rivers and forests. Smaller birds such as black poll warblers must migrate at night to avoid predators. Having no GPS or maps, the birds rely on the stars, wind, the magnetic pull of the earth, and smells in the air as their guides.

NONSTOP Flight

SOME BIRDS HAVE NO LAYOVERS in their migrations. So, like athletes, they have to bulk up. The black poll warbler flies from Alaska and Canada to New England in the late summer. There, it gathers in flocks and eats till it doubles its weight. Then in the fall, the small bird begins a 2,000-mile nonstop flight over the Atlantic Ocean to South America, which it completes in about three days. To accomplish a similar feat, humans would have to run four-minute miles for eighty hours straight.

Bad Timing: Everybody knows that the early bird gets the worm—but insects are now hatching earlier because of climate change. If migrating bird eggs hatch too long after the insect eggs, the birds will have a hard time finding food for their babies.

XOXO, Gossip Bird

CROWS TEND TO STAY PUT during the winter, flocking together in noisy groups of up to one million. They do this because they are all after the same food, and there is strength in numbers. If one crow hears something and flies away, others can follow. During the day, the crows forage for food. In the evening, they gather in the trees and shoot the breeze. They talk much like people, taking turns and not interrupting. So what exactly are they discussing? The best places to find food—a juicy topic indeed!

Good parents, skilled builders, talented musicians, and social, er, butterflies, birds really are just like us! And we are like them. Or, put another way, we are all birdbrains!

SAY WHAT?

bower a nestlike space built and decorated by a male bird for the purpose of attracting a mate.

brood to keep eggs warm, usually by sitting on them.

camouflage to disguise something so that it looks like its surroundings.

crop milk regurgitated food fed by birds to their young.

fecal sac baby bird poop enclosed in a mucous membrane.

flock a group of birds of the same species that are gathered together to eat, fly, or nest.

landmark a feature—natural or manmade—that can be used find one's way.

mate a bird of the opposite sex with which another bird has baby birds.

microbes organisms that can only be seen under a microscope; some are harmful.

migrate to move from one place to another at certain times of the year.

navigate to travel to a specific place using natural or manmade tools to stay on course.

predator an animal that hunts other animals.

nest a space built by birds for the purpose of brooding eggs and caring for young.

territory an area claimed by an individual or group.